Chakras

This In-Depth Manual Provides A Comprehensive Exploration Into The Seven Chakras, Specifically Tailored To Individuals Who Are New To This Subject Matter

(A Comprehensive Manual For Harnessing The Healing Potential And Positive Vibrations For Novices)

Alfonso Fabris

TABLE OF CONTENT

The Functioning Mechanism of the Seven Chakra Points within the Human Body.................1

The second chakra, commonly referred to as the Sacral Chakra or Sacral Plexus,......................15

The Heart Chakra 34

Factors contributing to an imbalanced Throat Chakra 91

Healing the Second Chakra................................. 104

The Wheel of Life....................................... 115

The Functioning Mechanism of the Seven Chakra Points within the Human Body

In the traditions of Yoga and Buddhism, it is believed that the human body consists of both the material and ethereal bodies, which operate autonomously, yet have the power to mutually influence each other. These conventions posit that akin to the sensory system, the astral body also encompasses an energy system consisting of 7 primary Chakra points that facilitate the flow of energy into and out of the body.

The seven points of the Chakra system can be found aligned parallel to the spinal column, corresponding to various aspects of both the metaphysical and physiological aspects of the human form. These Chakras are interconnected with the cognitive, physiological, affective, and transcendent aspects of the human body. Mastering the alignment of the 7 Chakra points can facilitate the cultivation of a healthier lifestyle and enhance one's overall physical and psychological well-being.

Each of the seven Chakra points aligns with a distinct portion of the anatomy and various psychological and emotional states. If you have become fatigued from studying the concept of parity, there is a reasonable likelihood that you can trace the cause to a state of discomfort present in one of the 7 Chakra points. "Allow me to elucidate the operating process in the following manner:

Fundamental or Foundational Chakra: Situated at the lowermost region of the spinal column, the Root Chakra is associated with the hue of red. This Chakra, being situated at the nadir and embodying physicality, pertains to all aspects of the corporeal and material realm.

Sacral Chakra: Situated approximately three inches below the naval, the Sacral Chakra is associated with the vibrant color orange. This particular Chakra is associated with our emotional states and the capacity to perceive and experience sensations in the tangible realm. It is also associated with sexuality, vitality, and reproduction.

The Solar Plexus Chakra is situated just above the naval region and is associated with the vibrant hue of yellow. This particular Chakra is associated with the somatic system and pertains to sensations of personal efficacy and prudence. This particular Chakra pertains to the faculty of volition and can be likened to Freud's conception of the ego.

The Heart Chakra is situated at the central region of the chest, adjacent to the heart, and is paired with the hue of green. The heart Chakra serves as the gateway that connects the realms of the physical and astral planes, making it a pivotal Chakra for contemplative practices.

Many contemplative practices incorporate the Heart Chakra as it aligns with feelings of love, forgiveness, and compassion. Activating the heart Chakra represents the preliminary phase in attaining the heightened consciousness and spiritual expansion provided by the throat, brow, and crown Chakras.

Throat Chakra: Situated at the posterior region of the throat, the Throat Chakra is associated with the hue of blue. The Throat Chakra governs the process of communication and self-expression. This vital Chakra can be activated through simultaneous conversation, particularly through the practice of specific breathing exercises and chants during meditation.

The Brow or Third Eye Chakra: Undoubtedly, the Brow or Third Eye Chakra holds significant prominence. It is positioned precisely at the midpoint between the eyebrows and is associated with the hue indigo. The Third Eye aligns with innate intuition, transcendental capacities, and the recognition of oneself. This particular Chakra exerts an influential effect on the sensory system and effectively facilitates the release of negative thought patterns.

Crown Chakra: The Crown Chakra is situated atop the head, extending beyond the physical body, and is associated with the hues of violet or white. The Crown Chakra aligns with transcendence, wisdom, and spiritual consciousness.

When the seven Chakra points are fully awakened and in equilibrium, it is believed that an individual will have attained a state of enlightenment. This is the goal pursued by many individuals who engage in the practice of yoga and meditation with a higher purpose, however, it is a challenging endeavor to attain.

The Significance of Chakras
The chakras establish a vital linkage between our corporeal form and our metaphysical essence. They regulate the

transmission of energy within the electrical grid permeating our corporeal form. The physiological network within our bodies bears resemblance to residential electrical wiring. It facilitates the transmission of electrical current across all regions, ensuring its availability for immediate utilization as required.

Every chakra comprises of principal organs and a collection of nerves that encompass our spiritual, mental, and emotional well-being. It is crucial that all our chakras remain open, aligned, and in a state of flow, as movement is ubiquitous. Once they encounter an obstruction, the passage of energy becomes infeasible. Consider it as akin to the plumbing system of a basin. In the event of a blockage, the water flow will be impeded. The aforementioned principle is applicable in relation to both our physical well-being and the harmonization of our chakras. Nevertheless, in contrast to household drainage systems, it is important to note that our chakras do not possess a tangible capacity for repair.

It is crucial to ensure the equilibrium of all our seven chakras, as they govern our thoughts and behaviors. They aid our body in countering emotional factors that give rise to illnesses, discomfort, and distress.

Emotional issues or stress have the potential to impede the flow of our chakras. Difficulties are prone to arise when the body's energy system encounters disruptions in its steady flow. The lack of consistent energy flow may ultimately give rise to physical ailment or displeasure. It affects everything, including our emotional state, breathing, metabolism and posture.

Dynamic or Blocked Energy Centers

Maintaining an unobstructed and harmonious flow of our chakras can pose challenges, yet as we cultivate mindfulness, the task becomes more manageable. Due to the intricate interconnection of our mind, body, and soul, an awareness of any imbalance in a specific aspect can effectively restore equilibrium in all other domains.

A considerable portion of the population remains unaware of the fact that chakras can exhibit excessive openness or stagnation. Retaining them in either manner is detrimental to their well-being. The unimpeded movement and blockage of chakras function as an energetic mechanism of protection. An adverse encounter has the potential to induce stagnation in the corresponding chakra energy, impeding its flow. Should we choose to retain or protract a sentiment such as culpability merely to avoid addressing it, we engender a state of inertia within a chakra, necessitating subsequent remedial measures.

The unrestricted flow of energy is initiated when we consciously activate and restore equilibrium to our chakras. Our objective is to effectively distribute energy within our physical being. It is imperative to ensure the equilibrium of our chakras and other energy centers within the entirety of our physiological system.

The Sahasrara, also known as the Crown Chakra:

The chakra located at the topmost point of the head, known as the crown chakra, has a perceptible influence that extends throughout the entire body and can even manifest in the hue of an individual's aura. This is a widely acknowledged phenomenon that has been recognized by numerous individuals over the course of several years, which accounts for the extensive interest in reading aura colors. Distinct chakras assume distinct roles in furthering enlightenment and exerting varied impacts on the physical and material well-being of the individual.

The designation of the seventh chakra is commonly referred to as the Crown Chakra. It is situated at the pinnacle of the cranium. In this context, we embrace the realm of spirituality, cultivating a heightened awareness of the interconnectedness that exists within the cosmic order. By means of this particular chakra, we are intricately connected to the rationality of every individual, thereby finding complete immersion within it. It is available in white or violet hue, symbolizing intellect, comprehension, and discernment of profound insights and fundamental verities. The chakra in question serves as a means of direct communication with spiritual entities and our elevated essence.

It becomes accessible at a later stage in life, subsequent to acquiring an understanding of the profound essence of our existence and developing the capacity to shoulder the obligation of serving both society and the environment. In the event of premature activation, there exists the potential for impaired functionality in another component of the energy system, which may result in transient sensations of confusion and indecisiveness. In the process of cultivating one's own capabilities, individuals exhibit a readiness to integrate profound spiritual principles and liberate themselves from egocentric tendencies. Individuals who adhere to a spiritual trajectory and do not have any religious affiliations can activate their chakra by aligning their experiences with its elevated principles.

The Western Perception of the Chakra System

The comprehension of chakras within the western hemisphere is a relatively novel notion. The initial scholarly reports regarding the subject matter did not emerge until approximately the Victorian era. Numerous mystics of the era eagerly embraced them as they sought to comprehend the harmonious connection between the physical body and the other realms of the spirit, striving to uncover their potential efficacy. Despite the recent emergence of this knowledge, it is being embraced by individuals in Western societies, enabling them to acquire the ability to harness their own energy and augment their personal strength.

The chakras have consistently served as a wellspring of resilience and enigma, enabling individuals to explore methods of harnessing their own potency and discovering their intrinsic fortitude.

The second chakra, commonly referred to as the Sacral Chakra or Sacral Plexus,

The Sacral Chakra, situated at the lowermost part of the spine and within the abdominal region, represents the second energy center within the human body. The Sacral Chakra is primarily linked to the region of your lower abdomen, encompassing the circulatory system, glands, and reproductive organs. Consequently, the focus lies on sensations and sexual expression. Therefore, when one's Sacral Chakra is stimulated and unblocked, they can effectively articulate their emotions without appearing excessively sentimental or overwhelmed to the recipient. You encounter no challenges in addressing and embracing your sexual identity, and you demonstrate a willingness to engage in romance and emotional closeness. Therefore, the Sacral Chakra assumes a prominent role in the emotions and sexual aspects experienced within your physical being.

If your Sacral Chakra is activated, you will likely exhibit increased receptiveness in expressing your emotions towards others, as well as being more open to establishing intimate connections. This phenomenon is highly commendable; however, it should be acknowledged that not everyone shares this sentiment, indicating a significant portion of individuals with a dormant Sacral Chakra. Individuals of this nature typically exhibit emotional detachment and present an impassive countenance in their interactions, as they tend to be closed-off to others. Contrarily, should there be an excessive activation of the Sacral Chakra, one would experience ongoing emotional intensity, potentially exhibiting a heightened susceptibility to emotions and a notably increased sexual drive on certain occasions. Moreover, a hypoactive Sacral Chakra may also give rise to emotional disturbances, compulsive conduct, and feelings of sexual shame. Consequently, achieving a harmonious equilibrium among the Chakras is a crucial factor in attaining a proper manifestation of emotions and sexual expression within one's life.

The Sacral Chakra is additionally connected to a mindset characterized by receptiveness and the capacity to collaboratively engage with individuals in our vicinity with a sense of contentment. Therefore, should the Sacral Chakra be in a state of equilibrium within your being, you would experience a sense of well-being, receptivity to novel concepts, affability towards others, and an abundance of artistic ingenuity and imaginative prowess. In addition, the activation of the Sacral

Chakra further enhances one's ability to effectively concentrate on personal objectives. Hence, the Sacral Chakra assumes considerable significance within the human body and, accordingly, it is imperative to strive for balance in this particular Chakra.

A properly engaged Sacral Chakra can also facilitate the assimilation of knowledge from personal encounters and collective wisdom, thereby fostering the necessary concentration to attain one's aspirations. On the other hand, an under-active Sacral Chakra would make you emotionally unstable and also may lead you to excesses in sex, foods and also drugs. In the event that an inadequate amount of energy permeates this chakra, one may experience symptoms such as timidity, bewilderment, and a pervasive sense of purposelessness. One can restore equilibrium in the Sacral Chakra by engaging in formal dance instruction, indulging in laughter, and partaking in meaningful social interactions with friends.

The Solar Plexus

Situated a short distance below the abdominal region, the Solar Plexus pertains to the digestive system, muscular structure, metabolism, and the nervous system with regards to the corporeal aspects of one's physique. The Solar Plexus serves as the cornerstone of your corporeal essence, enabling you to discern and comprehend the vibrations and sensations emanating from fellow individuals, objects, and environments. Furthermore, this encompasses the subject of self-reliance, self-discipline, and emotional concerns. Therefore, the equilibrium of your third chakra, namely, the Solar Plexus, will result in the acquisition of achievements and establish a state of relaxation and enjoyment surrounding said accomplishments. In addition, you will possess the capacity to effectively exercise your authority, thereby instilling within you a feeling of assurance and protection.

In addition, a dynamic and harmonized Solar Plexus guarantees a sense of self-control and adeptness in managing uncertainties. Undoubtedly, life would appear magnificent, consequently enabling the individual to enhance their concentration towards their life aspirations. Nonetheless, a disparity within this third chakra indicates an inequilibrium within either the initial two chakras, or possibly both. An adverse manifestation resulting from the disparity within the third chakra is the potential experience of gastrointestinal complications or malfunctions within the pancreas and liver, as these physiological aspects are intertwined with the Solar Plexus. Furthermore, in the event of an underactive third chakra, you might experience sensations of frustration and anger while simultaneously encountering challenges relating to power and authority.

Frustration arises from a state of diminished self-efficacy, and consequently, the insufficiently active third chakras are also linked to a lack of self-efficacy, thereby causing one to perceive tasks as excessively challenging to manage. It is imperative to acknowledge this vulnerability in the third chakra to potentially facilitate its restoration and achieve equilibrium. By gaining an understanding of one's weaknesses, individuals have the opportunity to regain control and progress in life while cultivating self-assurance. Hence, the cultivation of self-awareness assumes utmost significance in harmonizing the third chakra within your body, commonly referred to as the Solar Plexus. Conversely, should this particular chakra be activated within your being, you will possess a profound sense of self-assurance, thereby bolstering your potential for triumphant endeavors across all realms of existence.

Mindfulness Practices Targeting the Throat Chakra

The utilization of crystals is essential during chakra meditation. It is imperative that you utilize blue calcite or turquoise or lace agate and firmly grasp it with your left hand in order to facilitate the reception of the crystal's energy during the practice of meditation. In order to engage in meditation and direct your attention to the Throat Chakra, located at the base of the throat, it is necessary for you to assume a kneeling position. Additionally, one may engage in meditation and focus one's attention on the throat area, concurrently positioning a crystal on the corresponding chakra. Additionally, one may utilize essential oils believed to be associated with the Throat Chakra, namely rosemary, lavender, German Chamomile, hyssop, and Frankincense.

Third-Eye Chakra Mediation

Please assume an upright posture, ensuring your spine is aligned and your legs are crossed in a comfortable manner. You have the option of occupying either a chair or the floor. Place your hands gently on your knees and ensure that your chest is fully expanded. Place your tongue in a relaxed position on the lower part of your mouth, specifically resting it behind your frontal teeth. It is imperative that your index finger makes contact with your thumb, followed by the deliberate and unhurried act of deep, measured, and seamless inhalation. Direct your complete concentration towards the Third Eye, and in case any other thoughts occur, redirect them towards the Third Eye.

Engage in the meditation practice for a duration of 10 to 20 minutes, simultaneously articulating in a quiet or audible manner, "May I attain lucidity and discernment across all aspects and pursue solely the verity." Allocate a brief period subsequent to the contemplation before proceeding with the remaining tasks of the day.

Cultivating mindfulness to activate the Crown Chakra

The meditation intended for the seventh chakra necessitates directing the flow of energy from the lower extremities to harmonize with the remaining six chakras. Please assume a seated position with your knees bent and your legs crossed, gently closing your eyes afterwards. Visualize the potent vitality emanating from the crown of your head, accompanied by a luminous spherical illumination that progressively expands with each deep inhalation. The energy will begin to flow within you, potentially causing you to momentarily detach from your physical existence, as your concentration centers on elevating the energy towards your crown.

Additionally, you will begin to experience a subtle sensation akin to a tingling feeling on the topmost part of your head once the energy ball has grown to a significant size. At this juncture, envision the harmonious movement of energy coursing through the entirety of the body. Following the meditation session, you will experience a profound sense of alleviation, as well as a heightened synergy encompassing your physical well-being, mental faculties, and spiritual essence.

The Fundamental Vibrations of the Muladhara Chakra

The foundational resonance of the Muladhara chakra is denoted by the phonetic manifestation of 'lam.' This energy center is characterized by the presence of four delicate petals, each of which presides over distinct primal urges or emotional states. These floral segments are commonly referred to as the 'dharma,' representing the lowermost petal; 'artha,' signifying the petal situated on the right-hand side; 'kama,' denoting the uppermost petal;

and 'moksha,' symbolizing the petal positioned on the left-hand side. Additionally, each of them possesses a fundamental phonetic quality that, when vocalized, enables the activation of the inherent energies they encompass. The underlying phonetic form of 'dharma' is 'va,' 'artha' is 'sha,' 'kama' is 'sha,' and 'moksa' is 'sa.'

The inherent significance of the 'dharma' aspect lies in its alignment with the innate mode of cognition. Every facet of the cosmos possesses its inherent 'dharma,' an intrinsic yearning for mere existence. The 'artha' petal pertains to the cognitive mindset or psychological thought processes. Each sentient being within the cosmos possesses a cognitive yearning for the acquisition of specific information or the attainment of personal inquisitiveness. The petal known as 'kama' represents the tangible aspect. The term 'Kama Sutra' originates from the word 'kama', which denotes an identical meaning. Hence, this blossom symbolizes the yearning to satisfy one's bodily requirements. The inherent significance of the fourth petal, 'moksa,' pertains to spirituality.

A Root Chakra characterized by openness and equilibrium.

Individuals who possess well-aligned and harmonious root chakras typically exhibit a sense of tranquility and composure in their everyday activities. They experience a sense of safety, stability, and security in their professional and domestic spheres, undisturbed by any insecurities that might have manifested in their previous experiences. They exhibit no hesitation when it comes to unveiling their emotions and displaying vulnerability. They do not harbor any concerns pertaining to the security of their job or domicile. These individuals exhibit a state of being at ease and are inclined towards deriving satisfaction from engaging in constructive social activities and fostering robust bonds with their inner circle. This particular chakra underscores the significance of cultivating a sense of self-confidence and the capacity to experience a profound sense of connection and security in one's surroundings. Similar to the intricate circuitry within electrical devices that facilitates their operation, this particular chakra pertains to the significance of understanding and acknowledging one's origins. They will strive to guarantee a sense of security and foster the capacity to effectively navigate the challenges confronting us. Facilitating the unhindered flow of energy through this particular chakra will yield the comprehension of an individual's inherent susceptibility, prompting an examination of one's choices in an optimistic and productive way, culminating in transformative outcomes and the embracing of personal identity. In order to reinforce our self-esteem, it is imperative to affirm our significance and acknowledgment by reciting favorable, productive, and inspiring affirmations, such as:

- I am worthy.

- I am important.

- I am safe.

I possess a complete and indispensable nature.

- I am loved.

- I am currently situated in the ideal position in my personal and professional life.

An excessively active root chakra

An excessively stimulated root chakra exhibits characteristics such as an inclination towards materialism, avarice, and a strong desire for dominance. Given that this chakra pertains to the desire for material possessions and the need for control over significant aspects of one's life, an excessively stimulated chakra can prove profoundly detrimental in this respect. If an individual becomes excessively focused on material possessions, it will result in the emergence of manipulation and acts driven by greed.

An Impeded Root Chakra

In instances where there is an obstruction in the functioning of this particular chakra, individuals tend to retreat inwardly, seeking solace and relief by engaging in substance abuse, ultimately culminating in addiction and a sense of diminished self-worth and insignificance. Moreover, individuals who possess a deficient or obstructed Muladhara experience a multitude of concerns arising from apprehension and distress. Their concern primarily centers around the lack of safety in their surroundings, combined with the chaotic state of their financial situation. This individual may experience health concerns pertaining to the lower extremities, specifically the legs, knees, and feet, as well as potential conditions affecting the circulatory system, gastrointestinal tract, or skeletal structure. Individuals whose Muladhara is obstructed may exhibit a higher inclination to frequently change residences, as they lack a profound sense of connection and rootedness to any particular location. They face difficulties in arranging their material possessions due to a corresponding lack of order in their energy levels. They might discover that their residential environment is disorganized and in disarray. Should the Muladhara be irreparably harmed, the individual's demise becomes an inevitable consequence, given that their fundamental source of stability and survival has been irrevocably compromised.

The Heart Chakra

We now proceed to discuss the fourth chakra center, which serves as the origin of Love and Interpersonal Connection. Referred to as the Anahata in spiritual parlance, this particular chakra is frequently utilized to cultivate harmonious connections with others, fostering a web of empathy and comprehension. Situated in the central region of the chest, slightly to the left of the anatomical heart, this chakra center is pertinent to the adjacent bodily organs on a physical level. Green is commonly associated with the heart chakra, although certain individuals also acknowledge smoky pink as a valid representation. Given that the element of air is the preferred chakra element, the resulting energy is often interpreted as a form of interconnectedness in a universal sense. Due to this rationale, the Anahata is perceived as the convergence site where the energies of Earth and Spirit unite.

Given its designation as the heart chakra, one might be astonished by its aptitude for governing one's capability to experience affection. The Anahata serves as the wellspring from which an individual's compassion, forgiveness, and acceptance originate. It fosters relationships founded upon robust, affectionate bonds and even enables judicious differentiation based on empathy. The heightened level of acceptance bestowed by this particular chakra could be regarded as one of the most valuable blessings imaginable, fostering a perspective that enables an individual to embrace the world with a receptive and compassionate spirit, appreciating the entirety of existence. This instills a profound sense of gratitude and appreciation for the world at large. This expression of gratitude serves as the crucial link that enables our profound affection for ourselves and the world at large to coalesce, leading us to comprehend our significance within the vast expanse of the universe.

However, even affection must attain an apt equilibrium, lest it transforms into an impediment. Jealousy stands out as a prevalent and widely recognized pitfall of human emotions, particularly within the realm of matters of the heart. Experiencing a strong desire for a possession or attribute possessed by another individual to the extent that it generates feelings of resentment towards that person can at times indicate an inherent imbalance within the Anahata chakra. Engaging in excessive servitude and unconstrained eagerness to please others, even at great personal expense, can also indicate imbalances within the heart chakra. An individual who tenaciously clings to resentments, refusing to grant forgiveness, is undeniably prone to experiencing imbalances in their heart chakra. Regrettably, the presence of an imbalanced or obstructed Anahata may contribute to physical discomfort in the vicinity, thereby hindering the optimal functioning of the heart.

To invigorate and establish equilibrium in this chakra, one must make a conscious decision to embrace amore-affirming approach. Cultivate a greater propensity for embracing individuals who possess divergent qualities or perspectives from yours. Acquire the ability to disassociate yourself from individuals and environments that exude negativity, so as to safeguard yourself from being influenced by their detrimental energy. Engage in regular excursions amidst natural surroundings and immerse yourself in verdant landscapes. Engaging in meditation outdoors can yield significant efficacy, as it harmoniously integrates the vibrant hue of green with the essential element of air, thereby multiplying its advantageous impact. Make a concerted effort to comprehend your significance within the broader context and allow your newfound purpose to envelop you, enabling you to devote your utmost effort.

The Throat Chakra
The subsequent chakra we shall discuss is situated at the central region of the neck and serves as the focal point for the manifestation of Expression and Communication. The Throat Chakra possesses a fitting title, as it beckons us to confront existence with veracity and

uprightness. The well-being of an individual is intricately connected to the sincerity with which they communicate their thoughts and feelings. This encompasses suppressed thoughts or emotions that have been repressed and rendered inaudible. On each instance that this transpires, you are effectively diminishing the well-being of your fifth chakra. This represents the primary obstacle when it comes to achieving equilibrium in your throat chakra; however, by acquiring the skills necessary to surmount this challenge, one will subsequently cultivate a greater sense of honesty and reliability.

The Vishuddha chakra is symbolized by the hue of sky blue and is associated with the elemental representation of sound. While the Vishuddha chakra is commonly associated with our creative expression, it also serves as a pivotal junction for the energy flow originating from the Muladhara chakra, progressing through the Anahata chakra, and traversing through the Vishuddha chakra. Consequently, any imbalances in the preceding energy centers will greatly impact the throat chakra. Consequently, your proficiency in conveying your intentions, emotions, and so forth. will prove more difficult. It is pertinent to highlight the profound correlation between the Sacral and Throat chakras due to the distinct roles they fulfill in fostering creativity. While the Sacral chakra serves as the focal point of creative energy, the Throat chakra facilitates the manifestation of that creativity into tangible forms within the realm of reality.

As previously mentioned, the chakra in question becomes comparatively delicate due to the limited space through which lower energies must pass. A couple of the frequently observed attributes arising from an imbalance are a diminished inclination to attentively consider the perspectives of others and an increased tendency to engage in deceitful behavior. The latter stance starkly contradicts the essence of the Throat chakra. Individuals who exhibit significant apprehension when it comes to public speaking commonly experience an imbalance within their throat chakra. Analogous to the fear of public speaking, individuals may encounter pronounced bashfulness or social alienation. A less common occurrence could involve a divergence from an individual's genuine life objectives and a sense of isolation from fellowships.

The initial course of action in restoring equilibrium to this chakra should involve the pursuit of balance in the preceding chakras. Once this action has been completed, if any challenges persist, it is advisable to endeavor to unwind by listening to a soothing melody while envisioning a serene azure sky. As previously noted, the nurturing of truthfulness and integrity in one's everyday existence will contribute to the thriving and development of the throat chakra. Actively engaging with others and attentively listening can effectively restore this chakra, provided one refrains from merely nodding off. An alternative way to express the same idea in a formal tone could be: "Strive to engage in introspection, delving into your inner self to elucidate personal truths, thereby attaining the realization of your most uninhibited and authentic self-expression." Assuming personal accountability and tending to one's own needs also contribute to the well-being of the throat chakra.

Yoga as a Method for Harmonizing Chakras

The process of practicing yoga has the potential to effect healing, equilibrium, and augmentation to the seven chakras that reside along the spinal column. This endeavor frequently necessitates dedication and perseverance, implying the need for a mindset of patience in order to attain success. One may initiate their journey by incorporating a brief daily regimen of yoga, with the ultimate objective of harmonizing and fortifying their chakras. This endeavor is poised to cultivate a heightened sense of energy, happiness, and tranquility, thereby fostering an enhanced quality of life.

Presented here is a comprehensive yoga sequence, intended to address the various energy centers, or chakras, within your body and promote optimal harmony and balance among them.

1. Select the designated area where you intend to employ. Please ensure that you select a location or area that is devoid of any disruptions or interruptions.
2. Make yourself comfortable. Wear loose clothing. Additionally, it is possible to reduce the intensity of the lighting and accompany it with soothing music. Once you have reached a state of comfort, proceed to position yourself atop the mat in order to commence the routine.
3. Commence with the activation of the Sahasrara, also known as the crown chakra, by transitioning into a posture resembling that of a downward-facing dog (Adho Mukha Svanasana) through either jumping or stepping your feet. Maintain that posture for a duration of ten breaths, bearing in mind that each breath constitutes a complete inhalation and exhalation. Experience an increased flow of blood to your head, thereby

promoting the unblocking of your crown chakra.

4. Please proceed to harmonize your third eye/eyebrow chakra (Ajna) by lowering your knees and assuming the child's pose (Balasana). Direct your attention to the space situated between your eyebrows and perceive the vital energy associated with the third eye. Maintain this position for the duration of ten breath cycles.

5. Proceed to restore balance to your vishuddha chakra, situated in the throat, by transitioning to a supine position and assuming the posture known as Matsasana, commonly referred to as the fish pose. Maintain this position for a duration of five breath cycles while focusing your attention on the throat area.

6. Proceed to release any emotional blockages by transitioning into a seated position, folding your legs in a crossed position, and maintaining proper posture to ensure your back is straight. Kindly shut your eyes and inhale deeply. As you take a breath inward, envision the inhalation delicately contacting your heart, and as you exhale, envision it gently soothing the heart into a state of relaxation. Perform this step a total of ten times.

7. Following that, move on to the activation of your navel chakra (manipura) by assuming a prone position and transitioning into the bow pose (Dhanurasana). Maintain this posture for a single inhalation while directing your attention towards your navel chakra. Take a moment to unwind,

and then proceed to replicate the action on two additional occasions.

8. Subsequently, proceed to address the unobstructed flow of energy in your sacral chakra, also known as Svadhisthana. While maintaining a prone position, kindly release your lower limbs and assume a supine position on the floor. Place your hands beneath your torso, assuming a posture reminiscent of a cobra in the pose of Bhujangasana. Direct your focus towards the sacrum as you maintain that posture for a single breath. Relax then repeat twice.

9. Lastly, achieve equilibrium in your root chakra (Muladhara) by transitioning to a supine position. Assume a reclined posture known as the corpse pose (Savasana) and experience a state of deep relaxation. Direct your

attention to the sensation of remaining stable and firmly rooted, for approximately a duration of two minutes.

10. Once you have completed the task, proceed to stand up gradually while rolling up. Gently join your hands in a prayerful gesture, positioning them in front of your chest, followed by a respectful incline.

Allow us to shift our focus to the soles of your feet:
Your lower extremities carry you to various corners of the globe, and you shall now have the opportunity to further comprehend their potency. Similar to how a root sustains and nurtures a plant, your feet provide sustenance and nourishment for your body.

The Potential of Footwork in Energy Healing.

The feet hold immense psychological significance in our existence, as they symbolize our connection to our immediate surroundings, the earth, and the unyielding force of gravity. On the physical plane, any imbalance in the feet inexorably impacts the overall equilibrium and functioning of our entire being. Zchutz

One can readily conduct a brief examination to ascertain the activation status of their foot chakra.

Activated Foot Chakra: The capacity to concentrate and experience a sense of stability. An additional indication is the sensation of the cosmos swiftly aligning the previously unresolved enigmas in your life and along your path.

Blocked Root Chakra: obstacles appear when trying to materialize your aspirations and objectives, resulting in a lack of favorable outcomes. Another corroborative measure is your inability to sustain concentration.

Activating the Foot Chakra: According to energetic principles, one can induce its activation by engaging in the practice of walking barefoot on natural surfaces such as grass, mud, or shoreline, thereby establishing a profound connection with the Earth. An alternative approach involves directing your attention toward your feet during the act of walking, although I must admit that this method does not appear to yield favorable results from my own perspective.

Does this imply that the foot serves as a conduit for the release of negative energy, indicated by an open chakra, analogous to a foot that has expelled all forms of negativity?

The Significance of Foot Power in Islam

In the Islamic faith, the act of prayer is comprised of three primary positions:

Initial position: Assume a stance with hands placed over the chest.

Second position: Engaging in a back bend while gently resting the hands on the knees.

In the third position, one is required to assume a posture of bowing down, wherein seven distinct points make contact with the ground - namely, the forehead, both hands, knees, and feet.

Now, let us direct our focus to the third position, which, in my interpretation, involves harnessing energy from various sources such as the universe, Allah, and Christ, while simultaneously expelling any lingering negative energy from the soles of our feet towards the earth.

The Influence of Your Feet in the Context of Chinese Medical Reflexology:

According to commonly held beliefs, the application of massage techniques and pressure on the reflex points situated on the feet can effectively facilitate the process of healing while also enhancing blood flow to various parts of the body. Isn\\\'t that powerful? Have you ever contemplated the interconnectedness and integration of your feet with all other facets of your physique? It has been asserted that blocked energies in the body can potentially be cleared through the practice of reflexology, and I implore you to direct your attention to this matter.

Are you able to perceive that all things are converging towards a single outcome? The foot serves as the primary conduit for the release of negative energies in the context of energy theory, while in Chinese medical reflexology, it is regarded as the locus of any blockages."

The seven chakras can be classified into two distinct categories. The chakras, situated within the upper region of our body, are reputed for their capacity to govern our cognitive faculties. There exist four individuals present in the vicinity. Likewise, the chakras located in the lower region of our anatomy hold dominion over our innate qualities and capacities. There exists a total of three individuals.

The subsequent list comprises the 7 established chakras to which our attention will be directed:

1. "The Muladhara or First Chakra

2. The Svadhisthana or Sacral Chakra represents the second energy center in the human body.

3. The Manipura, alternatively known as the Solar Plexus Chakra,

4. The Anahata, also known as the Heart Chakra,

5. The Visuddhi Chakra, alternatively referred to as the Throat Chakra,

6. The Ajna, also known as the Chakra of the Third Eye

7. The Sahasrara, also known as the Crown Chakra,

Based on the insights of pioneers and scholars, the 7 chakras function synergistically with the overarching purpose of fostering the physical and mental wellness of individuals. The chakras operate to establish a distinctive amalgamation and equilibrium of our cognition, emotions, and innate impulses. Based on our research, it has been observed that certain chakras exhibit underdevelopment or incomplete alignment, while others demonstrate excessive activity or near closure.

A state of harmony in our chakras is essential for promoting serenity in both our mental and physical well-being. Therefore, it is not recommended that individuals should strive for an equitable level of utilization for each of the seven chakras. Conversely, emphasis should be placed on attaining equilibrium to promote holistic well-being of both the body and mind.

The subsequent sections of our e-book will be dedicated to elucidating the process of attaining consciousness regarding our seven chakras, along with a comprehensive array of exercises and techniques tailored specifically to facilitate their activation.

Six: The Inner Vision

The sixth chakra in our system of energy centers is commonly referred to as the Third Eye. It is positioned superior to the nasal region, situated amidst the eyebrows. The Third Eye serves as the epicenter of one's intuition and consciousness. A harmoniously activated Third Eye allows for the reception and implementation of divine inspiration that permeates our authentic beings. The Third Eye's energy enables us to comprehend our essence as celestial spiritual entities inhabiting corporeal forms. It affords us the capability to apprehend the cosmos by means of our intrinsic faculties, and harmonize our emotional, physical, and intellectual aspects with our elevated selves.

Activating, restoring, and harmonizing the Third Eye cultivates a state of serenity and harmony grounded in enhanced clear-sightedness. It enables the restoration of pituitary gland function, granting us the ability to perceive, comprehend, and effectively harness the profound wisdom embedded within the fabric of the universe. We attain a comprehensive perspective on infinity and eternity, thereby alleviating our apprehension towards mortality and enabling us to relinquish our attachment to material possessions. The concept of telepathy and the capacity to access past lives has been linked with the activation of the Third Eye.

An obstructed Third Eye results in heightened susceptibility to the energies emitted by others, subsequently causing a diminished capacity for resilience and assertiveness, and fostering apprehension towards achieving success. The absence of Third Eye energy gives rise to an uncontrolled and fragmented persona. It hinders us from recognizing and striving to achieve our utmost capabilities.

An excessive abundance of Third Eye energy has the potential to transmute charisma into manifestations of demonic pride and tyranny. Excessive adherence to religious doctrines and a reluctance to introspect on the underlying sources of one's anxieties frequently stem from an imbalanced Third Eye. The apprehension towards undergoing disciplinary measures, along with a resistance to embracing rational advice from external sources, contributes to a paralyzing aversion towards change.

The Third Eye exerts its influence over our pituitary and pineal glands, as well as our cerebral cortex, visual organs, auditory organs, and olfactory organ. It serves as the central governing system for our physiological faculties of perception and cognitive deduction. It establishes a connection between the cerebral faculties and the cognitive faculties, as well as the visual and auditory senses with the intuitive capabilities. The impairment of auditory, visual, and cognitive faculties is closely linked to the disruption of the Third Eye.

The Third Eye serves as the hub for our emotional intelligence. It enables us to achieve a harmonious equilibrium between intuition and intellect, harnessing both conscious and subconscious insights to discern veracity from deception. It enables us to bypass subjective interpretations and make decisions based on cognitive clarity.

Indicators and Manifestations of Disruption in the Brow Chakra

Physical manifestations arising from an imbalance in the Brow Chakra encompass a range of health conditions such as headaches, sinus ailments, ocular strain, diminished auditory faculties, aberrations in hormonal regulation, and impaired visual acuity.

Emotional irregularities encompass fluctuations in mood, introspective tendencies, and unpredictability. You lack the capability to analyze your own fears, nor do you possess the capacity to derive knowledge from others. You dedicate a considerable amount of time indulging in reverie, as your mind possesses an exceptionally dynamic and vivid imagination.

Strategies for Achieving Equilibrium in the Brow Chakra

When the Brow Chakra is in a state of equilibrium, an individual experiences a heightened sense of clarity, enhanced focus, and effortless discernment between veracity and deception. You will readily and openly obtain wisdom and profound insights.

Ask the Universe

Kindly inquire your query and exhibit patience as you await a response, whether it is forthcoming immediately or after a considerable duration of time, potentially spanning days or even weeks. The response could potentially originate internally, from an external source, or be directly derived from the cosmos.

Keep a Dream Journal

Most of us dream. Only a limited number of individuals can recall their dreams with precision upon awakening, let alone comprehend the underlying meaning of those dreams. Maintaining a dream journal enables individuals to document their dreams and commence the process of interpreting them to extract the underlying messages they convey.

Meditate Often

Practicing meditation is a valuable technique for achieving mental stillness, and it can greatly assist in restoring equilibrium to your chakras, including the Brow Chakra. Direct your focus towards the region of the Brow Chakra during your meditation sessions.

Choose Indigo

Given its significance to the Brow Chakra, it is advisable to incorporate indigo into your daily routine. One is free to adorn oneself with indigo, embellish a room with this color, incorporate it into interior design, attire oneself in indigo, or utilize it as desired. Discover a rich hue of indigo that is captivating to your senses and initiate the enjoyment of this delightful shade. Introducing indigo into your environment will enhance your ability to direct your attention towards the Brow Chakra and its inherent objectives.

Learn to Relax

Gradually commencing at the highest point and proceeding downwards, endeavor to loosen your muscles. Commence by addressing the muscles surrounding your ocular region, proceed to gently close your eyes, subsequently release any tension from the muscles within your eyes, and finally induce a sense of profound relaxation within your cranial area. Please take a moment to unwind and maintain this position. Observe and make a mental record of any visual stimuli that may manifest within your consciousness. Descend, affording each muscle group the requisite consideration.

Use Daily Affirmation

It is advisable to engage in a daily affirmation practice. It is actually more desirable that you engage in the repetition of affirmations throughout the course of the day. We have provided you with several instances of daily affirmations, yet it is also within your capability to construct affirmations of your own.

I am prepared to embrace an unconventional reality as my personal encounter.

I possess a formidable capacity for imagination.

My intuitive faculties and discernment are robust.

I possess a comprehensive view of the situation and have a thorough understanding of it.

I am immensely pleased and satisfied with the current state of my life.

I aim to cultivate aesthetic appeal in my everyday experiences.

I will cultivate virtue and strive for excellence in every aspect of my life.

I will heed the guidance of my internal intuition, as it possesses profound wisdom.

I possess formidable cognitive abilities that I am resolved to employ for benevolent purposes.

My mind is open.

I am receptive to expanding my level of spiritual consciousness.

The Throat Chakra

Given that the larynx is situated in this particular vicinity, it is a logical inference that the Throat Chakra facilitates the liberation of communication, the capability to utter appropriate phrases, and exhibit sensitivity when expressing truths. This particular Chakra can become obstructed when an individual encounters challenges in effectively expressing themselves or struggles to articulate their thoughts.

The Sacral Chakra

This particular energy center can be found within the lower region of the abdomen, positioned a short distance beneath the navel.

What is the function of the Sacral Chakra?

The vitality of this core governs one's capacity to experience sensations. Due to its profound interconnection with one's emotions and senses, the dissipation of this energy is prone to occur when one's emotional well-being is compromised.

The hue that aligns with the sacral chakra is the shade of orange, or in the language of Sanskrit, Svadisthana.

The Impact of a Sacral Obstruction

An obstruction at this location could potentially cause detrimental effects to both your physical and emotional well-being. Regrettably, the association between this specific chakra and emotions and perceptions renders it susceptive to inadvertent self-imposed blockages, resulting from one's refusal to acknowledge a fervently desired or required aspect of their life.

An issue that emerges with the Sacral chakra is presumably a result of one's own actions, thereby rendering it particularly challenging to confront and address. On occasion, individuals may find it more convenient to attribute their challenges to their external environment or even to other individuals. However, it is paramount in this particular situation to confront and acknowledge the actuality of the situation.

What are the indications of an obstruction in the Sacral Chakra?

There are multiple somatic and mental manifestations associated with this type of obstruction. A discernible concern that could arise is the challenge of establishing emotional closeness within interpersonal connections. One might encounter difficulty in developing a deep, intimate connection with another individual, as well as in sustaining relationships that hold significant value.

Even the exploration of one's own innermost self can potentially give rise to significant challenges, thereby hampering the establishment of genuine emotional closeness with others. Additionally, should you encounter difficulties in cultivating self-love, it may prove challenging for others to reciprocate affection towards you.

Furthermore, there exists a correlation between the obstruction of the sacral region and the occurrence of eating disorders. These issues may arise when individuals experience discomfort within their own physical being or seek greater personal agency and control over their lives.

There exist three primary classifications of eating disorders, namely bulimia, anorexia, and binge-eating. However, it is frequently observed that individuals may exhibit the co-occurrence of two or more of these disorders (for instance, engaging in regular episodes of binge-eating while occasionally engaging in purging behaviors as well).

It appears that there is an escalating prevalence of these eating disorders, with a downward age trend in those being affected.

Furthermore, apart from eating disorders, an impediment in the sacral chakra could also be correlated with issues related to substance abuse and addiction. Similar to individuals with eating disorders, individuals may resort to substance abuse as a means of "self-medication" and striving for a sense of empowerment, only to find themselves ensnared in addiction and devoid of the autonomy they sought.

Individuals may turn to alcohol or drugs as a means of managing challenging life circumstances; however, doing so carries the inherent danger of relinquishing self-regulation and descending into a state of alcohol dependence or substance abuse.

Therefore, it is evident that the presence of a blockage in the Sacral region can yield significant ramifications for both the physical well-being and mental state of an individual. The act of suppressing challenging experiences and memories gradually may result in an obstruction occurring in this particular chakra center.

This phenomenon can lead to a self-reinforcing cycle wherein the obstruction itself induces behaviors that exacerbate the obstruction.

3: Determining the Presence of Chakra Imbalance: A Guide to Recognition

There have been instances when you may have experienced noticeable impacts, both on a physical and psychological level. This can be attributed to the fact that there exists an imbalance in your chakras. This segment will facilitate the comprehension of your potential responses in the event of imbalances within the chakras present in your physical being. One will observe that the presence of an imbalance in even a single chakra elicits varied responses.

Root Chakra

It was previously noted that the root chakra is situated in close proximity to the base of the spine, near the coccyx. If one's root chakra is imbalanced, they will experience significant adverse effects.

One will discover severe implications on their lower limbs and feet as a consequence of chakra imbalance. Additionally, it will be observed that your immune system is significantly compromised. When there is an imbalance within this particular chakra, it disproportionately affects individuals of the male gender, resulting in a greater incidence of negative consequences compared to their female counterparts. One may discover that an imbalance in this particular chakra can result in the manifestation of constipation.

This particular chakra primarily pertains to the adrenal glands, intimately associated with the activation of the fight or flight response during various circumstances. When this chakra is imbalanced, you may experience a profound surge of emotion that significantly undermines the efficacy of your responses. You will inevitably encounter a dire necessity to seek shelter and sustenance!

Sacral Chakra

This chakra consistently encompasses the realm of emotions and also governs the capacity for affection one possesses. When a disparity arises in the functioning of this particular chakra, discernible alterations in behavioral patterns shall inevitably surface.

You will discover that there has been a significant impact on your reproductive system due to an inherent imbalance within this chakra. You will notice that your hip and lower back regions have also experienced consequences as a result of the chakra imbalance. One may experience severe discomfort and be vulnerable to kidney-related complications due to the proximity of the kidneys to the reproductive system, leading to potential urinary issues.

You will discover that you have inadvertently inhibited your emotional connection towards your beloved individuals. It will become evident that you maintain emotional distance and encounter challenges in articulating your affections to others. You shall commence to experience apprehension towards emotions and perpetually inhabit a state of melancholy.

Solar Plexus Chakra

This chakra serves as a direct conduit to your creative energy, and any imbalance in its functioning may manifest as specific physical ailments. One may experience feelings of lethargy or weakness regardless of whether any activity has been undertaken throughout the day. You are likely to experience a significant degree of stress as well. Your gastrointestinal system may also experience some undue strain. Additionally, it is possible that you are experiencing ulcers, which could potentially give rise to more severe complications.

Additionally, you may experience emotional imbalances that could potentially lead to reduced self-assurance. As a consequence, your self-confidence will diminish, as you will start to scrutinize every decision you make in your life. One may commence self-criticism and even develop a profound dislike for their physical appearance and behavioral tendencies.

Heart Chakra

As previously indicated, this particular chakra is situated within the mid-region of your chest in close proximity to your cardiac region. When an inequilibrium arises within this chakra, one will observe a significant negative impact on both the respiratory system and the cardiac functions. It is likely that you will exhibit a susceptibility to cardiovascular diseases and may experience occurrences of stroke. You may experience respiratory problems such as asthma, bronchitis, or wheezing.

In the event of an imbalance in this chakra, one may experience an excessive fixation or preoccupation with another individual. You will experience an affection for that individual to such a degree that it will manifest as an intense desire. If the individual in question is deceased, it is likely that you may find yourself in an undesirable situation, possibly wishing for an alternative reality. It is likely that you will experience feelings of insecurity within the relationship, potentially leading to recurring thoughts about your partner's whereabouts. Additionally, you might experience intense feelings of envy and occasional outbursts of anger.

Throat Chakra

This chakra is located in close proximity to the throat region and invariably influences the surrounding areas if it attains a state of equilibrium. You may start to experience vocal cord complications and occasional thyroid gland difficulties. You may harbor some disparities in the production of this hormone. There might be instances where you experience discomfort in your vocal cords, thereby rendering it considerably challenging to articulate words.

In the event of an imbalance in this chakra, one may encounter difficulties in interpersonal communication due to a lack of self-assurance, thereby inhibiting the ability to engage in meaningful dialogue. Furthermore, you might encounter the situation where you are incapable of engaging in a conversation with anyone, be it about yourself or any subject matter. One might also start to contemplate the moral correctness of their actions.

Third Eye chakra

This particular chakra is located precisely amidst the area encompassing your eyes, and in the presence of an imbalanced state, one can experience severe impairments in their visual perception. One may experience a gradual decline in visual acuity and endure persistent headaches, rendering it difficult to maintain a state of tranquility. The proximity between your ears and eyes implies that any impairment that affects your eyes may similarly impact your ears. You may discover that your auditory function has been significantly impaired as well.

You will discover that there are certain discrepancies in the way your emotions manifest as well. On occasion, individuals may experience fluctuations in their mood due to a lack of certainty about their emotional state. One might eventually lose sight of their own vulnerabilities and consequently begin to scrutinize the shortcomings of others.

You might start to lose sight of pending tasks and opt to indulge in reverie.

Crown Chakra

It has been conveyed to you that this particular chakra is situated at the apex of your cranium. In the event that there are disturbances to this particular chakra, you may experience a myriad of psychological ailments. There is a likelihood that you may experience bouts of chronic depression. You may experience a noticeable decline in your ability to focus and concentrate during your work or study sessions. You may discover an increased sensitivity towards the environment and develop a propensity to strongly disapprove of any alterations that may have occurred within your surroundings.

You are also encouraged to engage in introspection and scrutinize your actions at every stage. Furthermore, you might begin to experience apprehension and contemplation concerning the individuals in your vicinity, and even ponder your own self-worth and position within the global context. Despite your exceptional competence, it is possible for you to harbor doubts about your occupation.

You will discover that certain characteristics highlighted earlier also apply to yourself. This does not denote that self-healing is not feasible. You will possess the capacity to engage in self-healing through the techniques elucidated in the subsequent s. You will be instructed on the techniques to achieve equilibrium within the chakras.

Opening Your Root

In the realm of Chakras and holistic wellness, there exists a spiritual condition wherein one or more of our Chakras undergo closure. In essence, this signifies a diminished operational efficiency of the energy node, resulting in restricted or severed energy supply to this particular location. Luckily, a state of imbalance is solely a transient matter, provided that we can duly recognize its onset and effectively rectify the discrepancy or bring about equilibrium. However, due to the distinct placement and influence on various mental and physiological functions, it is essential to adopt unique corrective methods for each Chakra. Furthermore, fortunately, addressing the remedies for each Chakra proves to be quite manageable.

Indications of an Enclosed Root

While there exist additional indications that manifest when the Root Chakra becomes unbalanced or obstructed, the following inventory encompasses the symptoms that are most frequently encountered and readily identifiable:

Alienation

Eating disorders

Fatigue

Immune related disorders

Poor sleeping patterns

Weight gain

Root-Opening Foods

A number of individuals propose that specific foods have the ability to actively contribute to the restoration of imbalanced or blocked Chakras. Specifically advantageous food options for rectifying a constricted Root encompass roots-affiliated vegetables:

Beets

Carrots

Potatoes

"You might also consider experimenting with foods and spices that have a red coloration, such as:

Apples

Cayenne pepper spices or Tabasco sauce

Red meat

Root-Opening Exercises

Furthermore, apart from root vegetables and food items with red pigmentation, there exist alternative physical methods to rectify an imbalance in the Root or to restore its blocked energy flow. As you will promptly ascertain, there exist several methods one can employ to activate one's Root. I have allocated considerable significance to this Chakra due to its name's connotation, as it serves as the bedrock for your spiritual and physical well-being. In the absence of an equilibrium within the Root, the entire Chakra system invariably deteriorates. Despite the abundance of diverse exercises available through a brief internet search that specifically target this region, certain ones have demonstrated notable efficacy:

AMBULATION: This Root-opening exercise is highly beneficial for individuals who lead hectic, multitasking lives, as walking is an instinctive and regular activity. Direct your attention to the soles of your feet as you engage in locomotion. Take note of the sensations that ensue when your feet make contact with, and subsequently detach from, the ground. Acquire the ability to acknowledge those fleeting instances wherein your feet are firmly established on the earth's surface, and duly contemplate on the aforesaid sensation of being firmly grounded. Engaging in STATIC MARCHING could serve as a beneficial variation of this exercise.

Occupying a crouched position: An individual with a compressed base level should seek to encounter the physical sensations associated with equilibrium and steadiness. Squatting, characterized by maintaining a grounded posture with both feet planted firmly and facing in the forward direction, accomplishes this very goal. The integrity of body weight distribution relies upon the lower extremities to elevate and lower it, with the feet acting as a steadfast foundation to facilitate equilibrium and steadiness. The WARRIOR POSE, a stance that may resonate with those who have dabbled in the practice of yoga, presents itself as a commendable postural option to explore.

VISUALIZATION: The phenomenon of closed Chakras can sometimes originate from psychological impediments. Fortunately, the utilization of visualization proves highly effective in addressing and overcoming these impediments, should they manifest. To enhance effective visualization, engage in mental contemplation of an object or concept that embodies the notion of groundedness, be it in a physical or symbolic sense. One might consider visualizing a mountain, as an illustration, as its colossal magnitude renders it an insurmountable and unyielding entity. Alternatively, one may opt to imagine a tree—a natural entity endowed with its own tangible roots that firmly anchor it to the Earth. Assume a stable stance with your feet planted firmly on the ground, positioned at shoulder width apart, for a minimum duration of 10 minutes. Engage in the mental exercise of envisioning yourself as the aforementioned object. Consider the profound sense of rootedness that you experience in relation to that particular object. Allow the sensation of being rooted to distribute itself throughout your entire body.

RECITE REASSURING MANTRAS: Frequently, an obstructed Root Chakra elicits feelings of insecurity. These sensations have the ability to command the forefront of our consciousness and exert influence over our every behavior, or they may exist in a more subdued manner, akin to the muted buzz of a running fan. Occasionally, these emotions may be imperceptible; we merely experience a sense of unease. Fortunately, there exists a viable solution. Reciting the expression "I am secure, I am resilient, I am in good health" provides reassurance of our present safety and aids in dispelling the prevailing negative thoughts within our consciousness.

Factors contributing to an imbalanced Throat Chakra

The predominant factors underlying such conditions are of psychological nature; however, it is worth noting that certain tangible physiological issues can also contribute to the obstruction of the throat chakra, such as an overactive or underactive thyroid. Regardless of whether the disruption occurs within the physical or mental realm, the result of an imbalanced chakra remains consistent.

"Presented herewith is a more detailed examination of select immediate contributing factors:

Telling Lies

In the realm of sensationalist journalism, individuals have traditionally asserted the cynical adage, "One should refrain from allowing the truth to hinder a compelling narrative." However, it is undeniable that even in our current environment of deceitful information and attention-grabbing headlines, the significance of truth remains intact. In accordance with the conventional principles of chakric ideology, the dissemination of untruths can precipitate a significant perturbation within the throat chakra. Falsehoods carry detrimental consequences not only for one's own being, but also for the well-being of others in proximity. However, the compounding impact of all those misrepresentations will predominantly manifest within the throat chakra.

Subjected to Excessive Critique

If you happen to be surrounded by individuals who excessively criticize you, be it a domineering parent, spouse, or companion, their presence can significantly undermine your self-esteem and self-confidence. Furthermore, and to a greater extent, should the excessively critical individual persist, your individual expression will be so stifled that your throat chakra will undergo complete blockage.

Childhood Trauma

The development of your throat chakra may be greatly influenced by any notable childhood trauma, be it verbal, physical, or sexual abuse. Similar to the metaphorical sensation of a constriction in one's throat, a significant portion of the distress and grief encountered throughout our existence becomes lodged within the fifth chakra, known as the "throat" chakra. Encountering such circumstances can understandably pose challenges and necessitate the implementation of multiple proactive approaches to effectively navigate them.

Overactive Thyroid

Indeed, it is true that not all factors leading to an impaired throat chakra stem from psychological origins; there are certain instances where the underlying cause is physical, such as an overactive thyroid. The thyroid gland, which is observable, holds the distinction of being the most sizable among all the glands in the human body. Additionally, it has direct connections to processes such as metabolism, weight regulation, and mood modulation. If there is an imbalance in your thyroid function, it can not only negatively affect your throat chakra, but also have profound impacts on your overall physiological well-being. It is imperative to promptly investigate an excessively active thyroid, not only in order to facilitate the balance of the throat chakra, but also to safeguard one's overall well-being.

Remaining silent

It may come as a surprise to many, but there are instances where choosing silence can result in significant repercussions. Despite the frequent admonition from your mother to refrain from speaking unless you have something positive to contribute, it is not always advisable to adhere strictly to this advice. On occasion, under specific circumstances, it becomes necessary to express one's thoughts openly, thereby asserting one's viewpoint to those in one's vicinity. Resisting the intense inclination to do so has the potential to lead directly to a congestion or obstruction in your throat chakra. In the event that you happen to witness a glaring injustice and choose to maintain a state of silence, the burden of your omission may persist within you, ultimately manifesting itself as a profound obstruction of your throat chakra.

Absence of clemency

Lacking the willingness to tolerate and accept others can deplete your vitality. A conspicuous absence of forgiveness can result in a significant obstruction of the throat chakra. Ultimately, it is essential to acknowledge that imperfection is inherent to all individuals, and the occurrence of mistakes is an inevitable part of human nature. And individuals who exhibit negative behavior towards you are not beyond redemption, but rather, they are imperfect individuals who require guidance and rectification. However, individuals commonly perceived as morally compromised often possess inherent goodness within. The individuals who exhibit negative behavior typically do so due to a lack of knowledge and are unaware of the extent of the harm they are causing. Shedding light on this matter, we need not search beyond the illustration of Jesus Christ on the crucifix, where he beseeched, "Father, forgive them, for they do not comprehend their actions!" This instance is frequently and justifiably identified as an exemplification of forgiveness. However, it is not uncommon for even practitioners of the Christian faith to overlook the true meaning behind Jesus' words. He observed a humanity that was lost, conflicted, and confused, and boldly proclaimed their profound ignorance of their own actions; had they possessed true understanding, they would not have proceeded as they did. This holds true for the majority of individuals in their daily interactions. Frequently, individuals inadvertently inflict harm upon one another, often without attaining full cognizance of the detrimental consequences they are engendering. Do not allow the actions of a few troubled, puzzled, and conflicted individuals to erode your faith in the entire human race, nor diminish your determination to extend forgiveness. Acquire the virtue of pardoning others, for there may come a time when you, in turn, require forgiveness, ensuring the enduring openness of your throat chakra.

The Initiation of the Third Eye ~ The Indigo Sphere

Commence by directing your attention towards your breath, with an emphasis on inhaling slightly deeper than your habitual breaths. The majority of individuals tend to engage in shallow breathing.

Relax your muscles. Please shut your eyes.

Direct your focus to the center of your forehead, eliminating all thoughts apart from your intention to activate your Ajna chakra.

Mentally visualize and maintain a mental representation of your forehead. Engage with the sensations of your skin, your bones; genuinely perceive the presence of your forehead.

I now request you to direct your attention towards your forehead, acknowledging the presence of your third eye located in the center of your eyebrows. Please retain this image in your mind.

Direct your attention towards this visual representation, taking a few moments to ensure that you are able to comprehend and form a clear mental image of this depiction. Upon initial observation, the eye remains closed.

You possess the inherent capability to unlock it. There exists an inherent aptitude within your being, a celestial force waiting to be harnessed by you.

Keep your focus directed towards your third eye, sensing the gradual accumulation of your positive energy.

Imagine a radiant ring of violet luminescence enveloping the ocular region.

While observing, you subtly guide the illumination towards initiating the process of activating your third eye chakra, effectively dissolving any calcification present in the area.

Maintain concentration, exerting your will to facilitate the awakening of your third eye. You may experience sensations of cranial pressure; inhale deeply.

Gently unveil your eyes in a deliberate manner, allowing sufficient time to observe and discern any distinct sensations.

I cannot guarantee the emotions or experiences you may encounter, nor can I determine whether they will manifest immediately or gradually. I kindly advise you to maintain a healthy level of skepticism towards individuals who make explicit assurances in this regard. What I can assure you is that undertaking this spiritual awakening will bring forth advantages and metaphysical talents. Certain individuals may encounter an intensified sense of intuition, a surge in creative inspiration, or the occurrence of a lucid dream. Some individuals may detect a gradual realization dawning upon them. The greater the extent to which you devote time to honing your ability to open your inner eye, the more profound your progress towards achieving mastery of the third eye chakra becomes.

Subsequently, the transformative effects it imparts on your life will invariably manifest. Spend a few minutes each day practicing this visualization exercise, and you will discover that the rewards you receive will be well worth the patience.

Healing the Second Chakra

The second chakra, also referred to as the sacral or Svadhisthana chakra, encompasses various aspects of our being beyond just our sexual and emotional realms. It encompasses our sense of satisfaction, creative abilities, and capacity for inspiration. This chakra serves as a source of dynamic creativity, particularly when fueled by emotional enthusiasm, the excitement of new relationships, and enhanced interpersonal connections. When the chakra is operating in optimal condition, it facilitates the establishment and maintenance of robust interpersonal connections, promotes self-contentment, and facilitates the process of emotional release when sentiments cease to persist.

Nevertheless, the improper functioning of this chakra gives rise to physical maladies affecting the bladder, spleen, kidneys, and sexual organs, alongside emotional disturbances encompassing jealousy, guilt, and obsession. Fundamentally, these visceral organs situated in the lower abdominal region primarily facilitate the processes of cleansing and deriving pleasure. Consequently, this particular energetic center pertains to our capacity to engage in and embrace the multifaceted aspects of existence, as well as our capacity to transition and progress.

The following fragrances are associated: Damiana, gardenia, and orris root.

Related glandular system: Sexual

Musical note: D

Associated sound: [o] (pronounced as in the word 'home')

Herbs that are associated with this category include coriander and fennel.

Element: Water

Gemstones: Amber, citrine, gold topaz, moonstone, calcite, gold, coral, and carnelian.

Color: Orange

Healing exercises:

Pelvic thrusts

Yoga (cobra pose)

Healing foods:

Any items of an orange hue, including but not limited to oranges, tangerines, and clementines.

Cuisine with subtle spices, a variety of nuts, and seeds

THE INTERPLAY OF CHAKRAS AND THE AYURVEDIC APPROACH

Similar to how energy flows through the chakras, Ayurveda, an ancient Indian medicinal practice, perceives the human body as a microcosm, mirroring the perspective of traditional Chinese medicine. Additionally, it is observed that the human body comprises of the five interdependent elements, namely Water, Fire, Air, Earth, and Ether, which play a significant role in determining an individual's Dosha. Optimal health is contingent upon attaining equilibrium among these components and facilitating a smooth flow of energy throughout the body. Conversely, an inequilibrium or inadequate flow of energy will have an adverse impact on one's overall well-being. The essence of the companion's art lies in the restoration of the body's and energy's inherent self-regulation phenomenon, thereby facilitating the patient's reestablishment of their innate equilibrium and initiating the body's journey towards recovery.

THE PARAMOUNT IMPORTANCE OF MAINTAINING BALANCED SACRAL CHAKRA ENERGY

The sanctified energy center, positioned beneath the navel, is frequently associated solely with matters of sexuality. This box does not fully align with it. Naturally, it serves as the regulator of the reproductive systems pertaining to the female species, encompassing organs such as the ovaries, uterus, and so forth. However, it also encompasses the emotional core of the entire organism, consolidating approximately 80% of subconscious cognitions. When the sacred chakra is obstructed, various manifestations arise, such as impaired interpersonal connections, bewilderment, overwhelming emotional states, and more. In a state of equilibrium, this chakra serves as a sanctuary, characterized by its remarkably secure nature and heightened level of activity within the body. With this firm basis established, we can progress in life with increased vitality and elation.

RECALL ON THE CHAKRAS

In the Buddhist and Hindu principles, the chakras encompass the physical body, serving as a protective sheath. They operate as a unified system, wherein each of the seven elements must maintain its position and fulfill its designated role. They constitute an integral component of a unified entity. Due to this rationale, it is recommended that in the event of a potentially obstructed chakra, one should refrain from individualizing it as it is an integral component of a larger entity.

Ayurvedic medicine employs the use of chakras as a means to treat ailments, both physical and psychological in nature. Their objective is to assess the condition and conduct of a chakra, in conjunction with its interactions with other chakras. If an imbalance occurs, there will be a range of symptoms. It is highly probable that the chakra that is "stuck" is merely an incidental casualty of one of its adjacent counterparts.

In the event of chakra hyperactivity, which specific region of the body or mind does it select as the recipient of its excessive energy discharge? If, on the contrary, he demonstrates a lack of activity, he will seek alternative sources to compensate for what he is lacking and attempt to engage in productive tasks.

He siphons energy from his neighboring chakras, particularly the solar plexus which brims with vitality. An imbalanced chakra destabilizes our connection with the world, prompting us to seek sustenance by depleting the vitality of others through energetic assimilation.

The arrangement of these miniature vortices is thus crucial. Particularly when it pertains to the revered chakra.

The sanctified energy center, concealed within the utmost seclusion of the human physique:

The kundalini symbolizes a serpent, which is believed to be coiled along the spinal column and intertwined with the chakras. He embodies vitality and energy in every aspect. This serpent derives its origin not from the root chakra, as one might presume given its primacy, but rather from the sacred chakra. Hence, restoring equilibrium to this particular chakra takes precedence.

The sanctified energy center known as the Svadhisthana, or sacred chakra, is intricately intertwined with the elemental essence of water. It exerts its influence on the reproductive organs and the small intestine. It harmonizes the facets of sexuality, longing, artistic expression, and a manifestation of self-worth. Per the tenets of Hinduism and Buddhism, when we align ourselves with the correct course, it emanates a radiant aura, imbuing vitality. In the event of obstruction, an emotional imbalance ensues, characterized by discernible inclinations towards intense anger that seemingly arises without provocation.

At a physiological level, potential manifestations encompass urinary disorders, renal complications, as well as discomfort in the lower back. Numerous practitioners of yoga correlate this particular chakra with the concept of personal domain, as the majority of our subconscious cognitions originate within its realm. We align ourselves with the prevailing notion that a urinary infection arises as a consequence of perceiving a perceived threat within its intimate domain.

On the chakra pathway connecting them, once the root chakra fulfills our essential needs for survival, it then becomes the sacred chakra's role to bring the puzzle to its full completion. It elicits a sense of gratification in one's existence, bestowing enjoyment devoid of any moral qualms. In the event of his strength, it becomes evident that we are bestowed with a secure sanctuary within. We can strive to lead a life of utmost comfort and contentment. The hue of the object is orange, which is a fusion of the vibrant tones of red symbolizing the root chakra, and the luminous shades of yellow signifying the solar plexus chakra. This hue is associated with fervor, with vitality. She has the ability to dispel or alleviate somber emotions.

The vitality and exuberance of the sacred chakra is of utmost significance.

The strength of our romantic bonds is intricately intertwined with the sanctity of this divine energy center. This principle similarly extends to the significance we attribute to moments devoted to leisure and enjoyment. Without succumbing to boundless hedonism, it is possible to deliberately allocate time to engage in activities that bring us contentment.

The Wheel of Life

The term 'chakra' originates from the Sanskrit word that signifies a circular object or structure. When rendered verbatim from Hindi, it denotes the concept of a 'Wheel of spinning Energy', akin to a swirling vortex or an expansive reservoir of boundless energy.

There are a total of seven energy centers present in our physical bodies. Conceive of chakras as imperceptible, replenishable sources of energy. They are responsible for harnessing the cosmic energy present in the atmosphere, similar to how our residences are connected to a centralized electrical grid in urban areas. The only distinction lies in the fact that this cosmic energy source is readily available without any cost. Consider envisioning a vertical power current resembling a fluorescent tube that extends along the length of the spinal column, starting from the top of the head and reaching all the way down to the lower back. This energy conduit serves as our primary source of vitality.

The seven chakras are situated in the core of our physical self and are harmoniously positioned along this axial "power conduit." The chakras serve as the link between our spiritual entities and your physical body. They oversee the control and distribution of energy within the corporal entity. On occasion, the obstruction of chakras may occur as a result of heightened stress, emotional turbulence, or physical infirmities. Consequently, this disruption of energy flow leads to detrimental health implications, feelings of unease, and a sense of cognitive and emotional disharmony.

Chanting verses imbued with higher frequencies, known as chakra mantras, facilitate the purification of our energy centers. As a result, we not only endure but truly excel, thus enabling us to optimize our physical existence and instigate beneficial transformations in our physical, emotional, mental, and spiritual domains. In the realm of spiritual and therapeutic practices, as well as within the domain of complementary medicine, the term 'Chakra' frequently arises.

Chakra System Explained

The seven Chakras serve as the focal points for the flow of energy throughout our bodies.

The Crown Chakra

With a hue reminiscent of violet, this entity finds its abode atop our cranium, intertwined with the cerebral cortex, central nervous system, and the pituitary gland. It demonstrates profound understanding and encompasses a wealth of knowledge, receptiveness, and profound happiness. Reportedly, it serves as the link connecting us to the transcendental realm, the central energy point representing divine intention and individual fate. An obstruction within the crown chakra can result in psychological disarray.

The Third Eye

With its hue resembling indigo, this Chakra is situated at the focal point of our forehead, precisely between the eyebrows. It serves as a valuable tool when exploring the inherent spirituality of our existence. It represents the chakra associated with inquiry, cognition, and awareness. It is linked with the faculties of intuition and wisdom. The Chakra houses the aspirations of our existence in this lifetime as well as the recollections of our past lives. Encumbrance within the Third Eye, presenting as a deficiency in anticipation, cognitive rigidity, biased recollection, and melancholia.

The Throat Chakra

With its hue ranging from blue to turquoise, it is situated in the vicinity of the throat. It serves as the energetic center responsible for facilitating communication, fostering creativity, enabling self-expression, and facilitating discernment. It is linked to our cervical region, upper extremities, thyroid gland, and parathyroid glands. It pertains to the faculties of intrinsic and extrinsic auditory perception, the amalgamation of concepts, the process of recuperation, metamorphosis, and refinement. A blockage in the Throat Chakra may give rise to impediments in the expression of creativity, inclination towards deceit, or difficulties in effectively articulating personal desires.

The Heart Chakra

The hue of green resides within our chest's core, serving as the repository for affection, benevolence, unity, and serenity. It is widely held among Asians that the soul is situated within this location. This particular chakra is related to the respiratory system, cardiovascular system, upper limbs, and the thymus gland.

Romantic connections are formed by the activation of our heart chakra, as feelings of boundless love progress along the emotional axis commonly referred to as the solar plexus, before ultimately manifesting in the sexual center or Base Chakra. It is at this point that intense emotions of attraction are often experienced. When these energies transition into the Base Chakra, there may be an inclination towards matrimony and establishing a stable domestic life. An obstruction within the Heart Chakra gives rise to a decelerated functioning of the immune system, leading to ailments of the lungs and heart. Furthermore, it manifests in a display of inhumane conduct, a deficiency in compassion, and a proclivity towards deceitfulness.

The Solar Plexus

It is of a hue resembling yellow, situated at a distance of a few inches above the abdominal region known as the solar plexus, and holds connections with our gastrointestinal system, muscular structure, pancreas, and adrenal glands. It serves as the foundation of our sense of self, as sentiments of individual authority, happiness, and wrath are intricately connected to this core. The repository of our sensitivity, drive, and capacity to achieve is housed within this location. An obstruction in the Solar Plexus region may give rise to emotions such as anger, frustration, and a sense of uncertainty or perceived victimization.

The Sacral Chakra

The color orange is situated in the region between the coccyx and the umbilicus. It is correlated with the lower abdominal region, the kidneys, the bladder, the circulatory system, as well as the reproductive organs and glands. It is additionally associated with emotions. This chakra is linked to the notions of longing; gratification, sensuality, reproduction, and innovation. Blockage can manifest as emotional disturbances, patterns of compulsive or obsessive conduct, and feelings of guilt related to sexuality.

The Root Chakra

Colored in red, it is located in the perineum, situated at the base of the spine, and is linked to the lower limbs, skeletal system, colon, and adrenal glands. It regulates our autonomic response of fight or flight. It is situated in close proximity to the earth, with its functionality intricately intertwined with the preservation and sustenance of the physical self. The presence of blockage in the Root Chakra leads to manifestations such as animalistic instincts, heightened states of paranoia, fear, procrastination, and defensiveness.

Within this , a comprehensive analysis will be conducted on the seven primary chakras, elucidating the distinct functionalities associated with each. The seven main chakras consist of the crown chakra, the third eye chakra, the throat chakra, the heart chakra, the solar plexus chakra, the sacral chakra, and the base chakra.

The placement of the crown chakra is situated in the utmost position on the cranium. It is widely regarded as the foremost chakra among all. The crown chakra represents the ethereal energy associated with qualities such as reverence, enlightenment, faith, joy, and optimism. It represents the epicenter of all matters pertaining to the acquisition of collective, metaphysical wisdom and celestial insights. This can be achieved by practicing various forms of meditation and, naturally, by maintaining the purity and clarity of your chakra. Additionally, it serves as the portal to tap into the universal energy and adhere to its fundamental principles. Universal energy refers to the dynamic force that pervades every aspect of human physiology, perpetuating the vitality and functionality of cellular structures, bodily organs, and circulatory systems. There exist a total of twelve universal laws. These principles can be referred to as the statutes of action, the principles of divine unity, the doctrine of correspondence, the principle of attraction, the principle of causality, and the principle of recompense. The chakra in question pertains to matters of the emotions, specifically pertaining to sensations of pure joy, an individual's holistic link with matters of spirituality, and the individual's inherent sense of inner and outer aesthetics. This chakra symbolizes an individual's capacity to achieve a profound spiritual connection.

The location of the third eye chakra is situated on the frontal area, precisely between the two eyes. It is also occasionally denoted as the Brow Chakra. This energy serves as the focal point of psychic perception, allowing for the exploration of not only the present, but also the past and future, commonly referred to as clairvoyance. An individual can enhance this capacity by initially ensuring the purity and clarity of their chakra, followed by becoming proficient in the art of meditation, an accomplishment attained solely through diligent and extensive practice.

The third eye chakra is capable of perceiving both one's internal and external environments with utmost clarity. A significant proportion of individuals fail to recognize the dual nature of our existence, wherein the paramount emphasis ought to be placed upon achieving proficiency within the realm of one's inner being rather than expending excessive energy on external matters. The inner worlds of individuals vary from one another. The external realm primarily comprises a superficial, materialistic sphere consisting of objects, occupations, individuals, and the manner in which one is perceived by these individuals. Your intrinsic reality, nevertheless, comprises your individual cogitations, convictions, and principles. Your internal realm encompasses all the constituents that define your individuality. A considerable number of individuals lead lives wherein their internal realm is primarily an immediate response to the external environment and the events taking place therein. By cultivating mental discipline, individuals can acquire the ability to exert influence on the external environment through maintaining mastery over their internal realm, particularly their cognitive processes characterized by constructive thinking patterns as opposed to passive and negative thoughts. The cognitive concerns addressed by this energy encompass sagacity, creativity, perceptiveness, and the capacity to thoroughly grasp concepts and exercise sound judgment. This particular chakra grants individuals the capacity to perceive the broader perspective.

The throat chakra serves as the focal point for communication and self-expression, and it is situated in proximity to the throat area. The manner in which an individual harnesses this chakra determines the way they express their inherent essence and inner authenticity outwardly to the world. The amalgamation of your inherent essence and inner veracity constitutes your personal identity. One can utilize the throat chakra as a means to establish a connection or conduit between their internal realm and the external world. It is this inherent vitality that confers upon an individual the capacity to communicate with utmost efficacy.

The heart chakra serves as the focal point for all aspects of interpersonal connections and interactions. Engaging in acts of affection and receiving affection, as well as the act of cultivating, demonstrating, and experiencing forgiveness towards individuals who have caused harm to you. The anatomical positioning of this structure is situated within the thoracic region, precisely positioned superior to the heart. This chakra is responsible for endowing individuals with the capacity to experience love towards others.

The solar plexus chakra can be found situated within the upper abdominal region. It serves as the focal point of one's vitality, which exhibits a direct correlation with an individual's assurance, sense of value, self-regard, and inherent strength. It is the inherent vitality that empowers individuals to experience assurance and exercise authority over their existence.

The sacral chakra is situated within the pelvic region. It serves as the focal point of energy that facilitates the evaluation and management of your interpersonal relationships with fellow individuals. This energy is also interconnected with the entirety of external power. These are examples of conditions such as addictive behaviors, fixations, power dynamics, sexual impulses, and financial preoccupations, all distinct factors that might hold a significant influence over oneself. Additionally, this chakra facilitates individuals in cultivating the capacity to embrace both others and novel encounters.

The root chakra epitomizes the most rudimentary form of energy. It is situated at the lowermost part of the vertebral column. This central hub of vitality directs its attention towards the diverse fundamental necessities for survival. In order to ensure survival, it is imperative for a human being to fulfill a set of five fundamental requirements. The aforementioned elements pertain to air, water, sustenance, dwelling, and rest. The root chakra is also responsible for addressing security needs in their fundamental aspects, encompassing physical well-being, monetary stability, and familial connections. This surplus of chakra energy serves as the embodiment of an individual's fundamental stability, imparting a profound sense of being firmly anchored.

Melodies For Achieving Chakra Harmony, Restoration, And Purification

It is truly remarkable how music can be employed to harmonize one's chakras. There are two methods by which the fifth chakra can be effectively healed through the use of music: "

#1 Absorbing auditory stimuli through one's preferred musical composition, sacred utterances, and resonant crystal vessels.

#2 Emitting sound vibrations through the practice of chanting, reciting mantras, and utilizing seed sounds.

One can achieve a complete alleviation of stress through the utilization of sacred therapeutic sounds, commonly known as brain music. These meticulously crafted tones and frequencies hold significant efficacy in facilitating both the healing process and the harmonization of one's chakras, ultimately inducing a state of profound tranquility and inner equilibrium.

The music aids in the alleviation of vibrational obstacles and any forms of resistance, ultimately resulting in a profound sense of inner tranquility experienced by the listener.

Certain artists, such as Gordon, possess the expertise to craft music that can foster healing on a holistic level, encompassing the physical, mental, and spiritual dimensions. They achieve this through the process of crafting songs in a meditative state, thereby allowing these compositions to effectively encompass and reflect the individual energies associated with each of the 7 chakras. For enhanced efficacy, the songs are subsequently categorized into two sections, offering the option to partake in either two brief meditations or a single lengthier meditation, promoting a more profound experience. Subsequently, you have the option to utilize the album as a modality for tranquil chakra meditation, thereby facilitating the emergence of brainwave meditation, or alternatively, as a therapeutic auditory accompaniment for sleep, reiki, massage, and yoga.

Yoga For Balancing Chakras

To achieve equilibrium, promote restoration, and eliminate blockages within your chakras, incorporating yoga into your routine can be a beneficial approach. Please bear in mind that dedicating sufficient time to practice yoga is necessary in order to attain the intended outcomes.

First and foremost, you can initiate the process by incorporating brief daily yoga sessions, eventually leading to the attainment of chakra equilibrium. The subsequent yoga sequences provided will assist in addressing each chakra point throughout your body and facilitate the achievement of harmonious equilibrium. Prior to commencing the routines, ensure that you have access to a sufficiently spacious, disturbance-free environment. Furthermore, it is advisable to don loose apparel that will induce a sensation of ease and well-being. Additionally, it would be advisable to lower the intensity of the lighting, if feasible, and create a calming ambiance by playing gentle melodies. Once all these arrangements are in order, position yourself on your yoga mat and commence the straightforward sequence of exercises.

Methods to Achieve Chakra Balance Through Yoga Practice

It is more advantageous to commence with the crown chakra. Commence by positioning your feet in a posture reminiscent of a canine assuming a downward-facing position (adho mukha svanasana). Sustain that position for a duration of fifteen breaths. You will experience increased blood circulation towards your head, facilitating the unblocking of your crown chakra.

Proceed to harmonizing the subsequent chakra, which corresponds to the third eye, by assuming a child pose (balasana) and gently lowering your knees. Ensure that you direct your focus towards the region positioned between your elbows, so as to experience the energetic presence of the third eye. Please maintain this position for a duration of ten breaths.

Continuing with the restoration of your throat chakra (vishuddha), advance by assuming a supine position and transitioning into a fish pose (matsasana). Maintain this posture for approximately five breaths, with a heightened focus on your throat.

Transition to unblock your heart by assuming an upright sitting position, with your legs crossed and back maintained in proper alignment. Inhale deeply and maintain closed eyelids. Continuously engage in the act of inhalation while concurrently directing your focus towards the breath, placing your hand upon your chest area. Upon exhalation, envision a sense of relaxation permeating through your heart. Reiterate the procedure a minimum of ten instances.

Upon completion of this task, proceed to the facilitation of the unblocking of your Sacral chakra, also known as manipura. This action can be achieved by assuming a prone position and transitioning into a bow pose (dhanurasana). Maintain this posture for several breath cycles while maintaining concentration. Take a moment to unwind and subsequently perform the procedure an additional two times.

Once you have completed this task, you may proceed to the unblocking of your sacral chakra (svadhisthana). Assume the aforementioned position, wherein you are positioned on your abdomen. Release the grip on your legs and allow yourself to recline horizontally on the floor, assuming the posture resembling that of a cobra in the practice of bhujangasana. Devote your attention to maintaining that pose for a minimum of one breath. Relax and repeat twice.

Once you have completed this task, you may proceed to restore equilibrium to your root chakra (muladhara) by transitioning onto your supine position. Attain the corpse pose (savasana) through the act of unwinding and allowing oneself to relax. Direct your attention and cultivate a sense of stability and groundedness for a minimum duration of three minutes.

Once all of these procedures have been completed, gradually rise to a standing position while bringing your hands together in a manner reminiscent of a prayer position, before subsequently performing a respectful bow.

Two: Nourishing the Heart Chakra through Dietary Measures and Physical Activity

Nourishment for the Heart Chakra" or "Culinary Options for Balancing the Heart Chakra

The heart chakra exercises jurisdiction over one's romantic endeavors and interpersonal connections. Maintaining equilibrium is fundamental in these facets of your existence. Hence, it is highly advisable to consume foods that denote equilibrium for optimal balance of this chakra. It is important to take into consideration that the color associated with the fourth chakra is green.

In the context of traditional Chinese medicine, green vegetables are commonly acknowledged as being neutral in terms of their yin-yang properties. These attributes render them highly suitable for facilitating harmony in the heart chakra, as they exhibit no discernible impact on equilibrium. Additionally, their coloration is in shades of green, rendering them harmonious with the fourth chakra. One can consume green leafy vegetables such as kale, spinach, cabbage, lettuce, and broccoli in order to restore equilibrium to the heart chakra. It is highly recommended that you consider opting for vegetables such as green peas, brussels sprouts, asparagus, along with a variety of herbs such as mint, oregano, parsley, basil, and sage.

Essentially, one may incorporate various types of green vegetables into their meals for this intention.

Furthermore, the heart chakra can be nourished by the consumption of various fruits, such as bell peppers, green olives, cucumbers, avocados, kiwis, green grapes, apples, and limes. Devise creative approaches to integrating lime into your dietary regimen.

Green tea, as well as beverages that include wheatgrass, barley grass, and spirulina, provide considerable advantages.

Consuming food items that are rich in energy content and contain pinkish hues, such as certain varieties of meat, can be beneficial. Keeping this in consideration, it is worth noting that salmon, pork, and prime rib can also be ingested for this intent.

The cardiac chakra grants us the capacity to bestow love and compassion upon others. If there is an imbalance in this particular chakra, the vitality of your heart energy may become diminished.

Nourishment for fostering love and compassion encompasses a variety of options, such as foods abundant in chlorophyll, sprouts, vegetables, any nutritionally dense foods with a prominent green hue, and uncooked edibles.

The heart chakra will also thrive through the act of distributing nourishment among others, expressing appreciation for nourishing oneself, and imbuing affection into the water we consume and the food we partake in during mealtime.

Dining with your dear ones is capable of enhancing the positive vibrations within your heart's chakra. If you are experiencing elevated levels of stress, it is advisable to refrain from engaging in emotional eating as the consumables you indulge in have the potential to become sources of comfort. It is possible that you might find yourself relying on it as a means of stress alleviation. Although this may offer some initial assistance and have minimal negative consequences, it might divert your attention from addressing the underlying issue of balancing your chakras and instead encourage reliance on temporary and ineffectual remedies.

Exercises

This particular chakra holds significant importance, contributing immensely to one's overall happiness and fulfillment in life. Hence, it is recommended that individuals of all ages engage in the prescribed exercises provided. There is no such thing as an excess of affection within one's heart. The most effective action to restore energy balance to this chakra is to cultivate heightened awareness of others, acquire empathy, and foster humility. Once you develop the capacity to expose your innermost emotions and thoughts to others, you will discover a profound sense of contentment. Exhibit sincerity and compassion, and maintain a pleasant demeanor towards individuals, even in instances where they may not necessarily deserve it. It promotes emotional healing and facilitates the process of transcending phases of negative experiences.

www.ingramcontent.com/pod-product-compliance
Lightning Source LLC
Chambersburg PA
CBHW050245120526
44590CB00016B/2223